A **TRUE** BOOK

Animals Helping at Home

L U C I A   R A A T M A

Children's Press®
An Imprint of Scholastic Inc.
New York   Toronto   London   Auckland   Sydney
Mexico City   New Delhi   Hong Kong
Danbury, Connecticut

Content Consultant
Dr. Stephen S. Ditchkoff
Professor of Wildlife Sciences
Auburn University
Auburn, Alabama

Library of Congress Cataloging-in-Publication Data
Raatma, Lucia, author.
 Animals helping at home / Lucia Raatma.
   pages cm. — (A true book)
 Summary: "Learn how animals can be trained to help people with household tasks." — Provided
by publisher.
 Audience: Ages 9–12.
 Audience: Grades 4 to 6.
 Includes bibliographical references and index.
 ISBN 978-0-531-21258-5 (library binding : alk. paper) — ISBN 978-0-531-21285-1 (pbk. : alk. paper)
 1. Animals as aids for people with disabilities—Juvenile literature. 2. Guide dogs—Juvenile litera-
ture. 3. Animal training—Juvenile literature. 4. Working animals—Juvenile literature. I. Title. II.
Series: True book.
 HV1569.6.R33 2015
 361'.05—dc23   2014030580

© 2015 Scholastic Inc.
All rights reserved. Published in 2015 by Children's Press, an imprint of Scholastic Inc. Published
simultaneously in Canada. Printed in China 62
SCHOLASTIC, CHILDREN'S PRESS, A TRUE BOOK™, and associated logos are trademarks and/or
registered trademarks of Scholastic Inc.
1 2 3 4 5 6 7 8 9 10 R 24 23 22 21 20 19 18 17 16 15

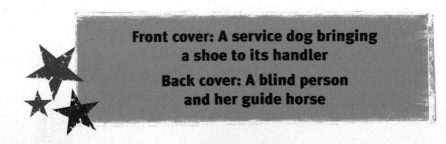

**Front cover: A service dog bringing
a shoe to its handler**

**Back cover: A blind person
and her guide horse**

Find the Truth!

Everything you are about to read is true *except* for one of the sentences on this page.

Which one is **TRUE**?

T or F Horses can help guide people who are blind.

T or F Dogs are never allowed in hospitals.

Find the answers in this book.

3

Contents

Capuchin monkeys help people who cannot move their arms or legs.

Support dogs assist military men and women.

Service animals often form close bonds with their owners.

CHAPTER 1

Animals Know How to Help

Every day, people all over the world benefit from the help of animals. In the United States alone, there are more than 57 million people who have **disabilities**. Many of these people rely on dogs, miniature horses, and monkeys to assist them with daily activities. These animals are trusted and reliable companions.

Dogs can help people with medical issues.

Americans With Disabilities Act

Service animals are specially trained to help people who need assistance. In 1990, a law called the Americans with Disabilities Act (ADA) explained what these animals do. They help people who are blind or deaf. They remind people to take their medicine. They help people with **post-traumatic stress disorder** (PTSD) remain calm. They help other people who suffer **seizures**.

A dog may have to disobey a command to keep a human safe.

A service dog is trained to help a young girl know when to take medicine for her diabetes.

Service animals are even allowed on airplanes with their owners.

Many of these animals help at home. The ADA
ensures that service animals are also allowed
in public places. This applies mostly to dogs
and sometimes horses. Some dogs are allowed
on airplanes. Others can go with their owners
to libraries, restaurants, and other businesses.
Service animals are allowed in patient rooms in
hospitals. However, they are not allowed in special
hospital areas such as operating rooms.

A guide dog's special handle allows the dog to provide clear guidance to its owner.

Guide Dogs

Guide dogs help people who are blind or have some loss of vision. These dogs assist their humans in moving around objects the humans cannot see. They help their humans stop at steps and then go up or down. Outside the home, they let their humans know where they need to stop at curbs and cross streets. A guide dog wears a harness and a U-shaped handle.

 Most guide dogs work for about seven or eight years.

Blindfolded trainers help teach guide dogs to navigate obstacle courses.

Training Guide Dogs

Many organizations train dogs to be guide dogs. These groups raise puppies to take on this important job. For a year, volunteers care for the puppies. Then professional trainers spend four months to a year working with the dogs. They teach the dogs commands and how to keep their humans safe. The trainers sometimes wear blindfolds to test the dogs' abilities.

Humans who are receiving guide dogs also have to be trained. They are taught about caring for dogs. They learn basic commands and how to hold the harness and work with the dogs. The people receiving the dogs agree to help teach the dogs new skills. They also have to know the laws about where in public their dogs are allowed.

Laws allow people to bring service dogs on public transportation even when regular pets are not allowed.

Labrador and golden retrievers are common breeds of service dogs.

How to Act With Guide Dogs

Guide dogs and their humans have a special bond. The dog listens for instructions and helps its human walk safely. Experts say the human is like a **navigator**, but the dog is the pilot. It is important that other people do not pet the dog or take hold of the dog's handle. A guide dog is a working dog, not a pet.

People should never distract a guide dog while it is working.

Morris Frank and Buddy

In the 1920s, German shepherds were being used in Europe to help soldiers who had lost their sight. Dorothy Harrison Eustis wrote about these dogs in the *Saturday Evening Post* magazine. Morris Frank, a blind 19-year-old American, heard the story. He wrote Eustis to ask for help in getting such a dog. He ended up traveling to Switzerland and being trained. He then partnered with Buddy, the first guide dog in the United States. Frank and Eustis went on to found The Seeing Eye, a group that still trains guide dogs.

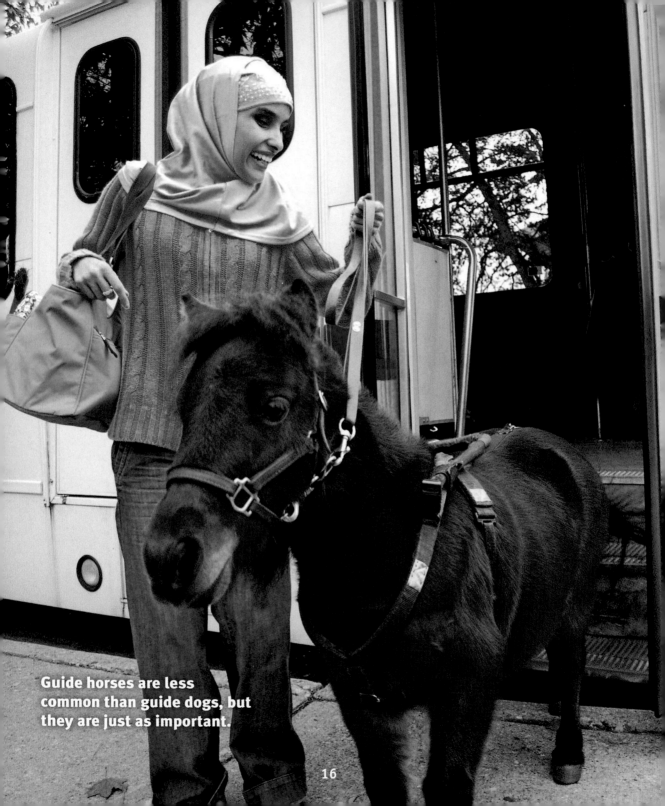

Guide horses are less common than guide dogs, but they are just as important.

CHAPTER 3

Horses in the Home

Dogs are not the only assistance animals that help people who are blind. Miniature horses also provide guidance to people with vision disabilities. Often, there are not enough guide dogs to help all the people who are blind. People who are used to being around horses sometimes prefer to use miniature horses instead of dogs. Guide horses are also good for people who are **allergic** to dogs.

Guide horses may live outside when they are not working.

Like guide dogs, guide horses are equipped with special handles for their owners to hold on to.

Training a Guide Horse

Guide horses are highly trained, just as guide dogs are. They can start training at six months of age. Before starting, the horses are tested to make sure they are healthy and smart. Then, trainers spend many months teaching them commands. The horses learn to follow their humans' commands and help them move from place to place.

Size and Sight

Guide horses are usually no taller than 26 inches (66 centimeters) at the **withers**. They usually weigh between 50 and 100 pounds (22.7 and 45.4 kilograms). Guide horses have an almost 350-degree field of vision. This means they can see almost all the way around their bodies without turning their heads. This range helps the horses keep their humans safe.

Miniature horses do not get nearly as large as their full-size cousins.

Guide horses can see very well, even in the dark.

DO NOT TOUCH
Service Animal on Duty

How Horses Work

Guide horses work in people's homes. They help them get around the house safely. They also help in public. Many guide horses are trained to travel in cars, on buses, and on subways. They can manage escalators and elevators, too, if needed. Most guide horses live in houses in rural areas. But they can adjust to living in city apartments.

Guide horses often wear small shoes to protect their hooves.

Owners often become very affectionate toward their guide horses.

Miniature horses can live to be 50 years old.

Like guide dogs, guide horses can become attached to their humans. The horses and humans are like a team. The horses stay with the humans and help them live safely. Most guide horses get along well with other animals, too. Their humans may have dogs and cats. Guide horses are not pets, however. They are never to be ridden.

Being a Person's Eyes

Have you ever thought about how dangerous it can be just to walk down the street? You have to stop for cars, avoid obstacles, and stay safely on the sidewalk. This is easy if you can see where you're going. But for a blind person, it's a challenge. This is where guide dogs come in.

The human holds the guide dog by the harness handle.

The guide dog stops at the curb.

The human listens for traffic and tells the dog when to go forward.

A sign tells people that a blind person lives in the neighborhood.

CAUTION
BLIND
PERSON

The guide dog helps the human move around a fallen bicycle.

Hearing dogs keep both ears open for sounds that are important to their owners.

CHAPTER 4

Hearing Dogs

People who are deaf need to be alerted to certain noises. Hearing dogs make sure humans know when a doorbell rings. They tell their humans when an alarm or oven timer goes off. The dogs also alert their humans to other important sounds, such as crying babies, ringing telephones, and smoke alarms. These dogs can save their humans' lives.

Hearing dogs often wear a special vest.

Most hearing dogs are small breeds.

Hearing dogs can alert humans within 15 seconds of a sound starting.

How Hearing Dogs Are Trained

Hearing dogs are usually small to medium in size. They can be many different breeds or mixed breeds. Terriers, Chihuahuas, poodles, and cocker spaniels are common hearing dogs. The best hearing dogs are energetic. They are friendly and enjoy being around people.

Volunteers raise the puppies for several months and help socialize them with other animals and people. Then, trainers teach the hearing dogs about important sounds. Humans who work with hearing dogs learn to use commands. When the dogs hear a certain sound, they make contact with their humans. Then they guide their humans to the sound. People who use hearing dogs are responsible for caring for the dogs and keeping them healthy.

Hearing dogs go everywhere with their humans, even to work.

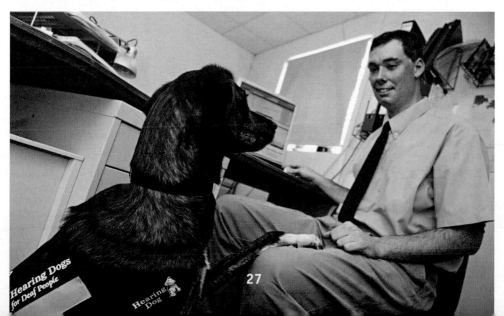

A helper monkey uses a cloth to scratch an itch on its owner's face.

CHAPTER 5

Helper Monkeys

When people suffer a spinal injury, they can become **paralyzed**. This means they are unable to walk. They may also be unable to use their arms or hands. Capuchin monkeys can help. Their amazing hands and flexible fingers assist people in many ways. They can pick up objects, push buttons, turn pages, and perform other everyday tasks.

Capuchin monkeys can live for 30 to 40 years.

How Monkeys Are Trained

Before training, monkeys spend the early part of their lives being socialized. They live in homes and become used to being around humans. When they are ready, they start training. They learn about the needs of paralyzed humans. They are trained to pick up and use everyday human objects. They learn to master refrigerators and CD players, as well as both electric and manual wheelchairs.

People are much less likely to be allergic to monkeys than to other animals.

Helper monkeys are rewarded for good behavior with treats such as peanut butter.

Monkeys can feed owners who can't move their arms.

Why Monkeys?

Monkeys are eager to help. They can develop a special connection with humans. They like caring for humans. They also enjoy snuggling and being affectionate with humans. They are wonderful companions in the home. They can help turn on the television or reach the telephone. They can insert straws into glasses or bottles. They can even position a person's legs in a wheelchair.

Dogs use special
handles to open doors.

CHAPTER 6

Other Ways That Dogs Assist

Guide dogs can help people who are blind and deaf. But service dogs can provide a variety of assistance to people with other medical issues, too. They can help people who are in wheelchairs. They can retrieve objects that are dropped. They can turn light switches on and off. They can also open and close doors.

Service dogs wear jackets, backpacks, or harnesses.

Seizure-detecting dogs stay by their owners' sides at all times.

Seizure Response and Alert Dogs

Many people throughout the world live with **epilepsy**. This is a medical condition that can cause people to have unexpected seizures. Other illnesses cause seizures, too. Seizure response dogs can help. They alert adults if a child is having a seizure. They do this by barking or pressing an alarm. If a person falls during a seizure, a dog can get between the person and the floor. This prevents injury.

Some seizure response dogs can become seizure alert dogs. This means they can detect that a human will have a seizure soon—usually within the next 10 or 20 minutes. This allows the human to get to a safe place, call for help, or take medication. Dogs can perhaps predict the seizure by smelling a change in the human's blood or noticing small changes in the human's movements.

Seizure alert dogs can help a human get up after a seizure.

A trainer simulates a seizure to test a dog's response.

Reaching People With Autism

Autism is a condition that affects millions of people. People with autism have a hard time communicating and interacting with others. They can become upset and confused in crowds or other noisy places. This makes it challenging to go to school or other public areas. Autism service dogs help people with autism manage everyday events.

Timeline of Helper Animals

79 CE
Wall paintings show a blind man possibly being led by a dog.

1929
Morris Frank and Dorothy Harrison Eustis establish the first guide dog school in the United States.

The dogs help their humans remain calm and focus on what is important. Autism service dogs are specially trained to accompany children to school. They can also go on buses or in cars. They are constant companions. They can guide their humans away from a loud situation. Or they may guide their humans to another person who can help.

1979
The first helper monkey is put into service.

1999
The Guide Horse Foundation is established.

A boy with autism hugs his dog.

Autism service dogs can carry notes when a person needs help.

People with autism can get distracted and wander away. Dogs can help find these humans and get them home safely. Autism service dogs can help humans remember important objects, such as keys or a wallet. People with autism can get upset easily. Just holding a dog and pressing against its body can help the humans stay calm. These dogs help people with autism lead less stressful lives.

Time to Take Your Medicine

Many people need to take medication for an illness or other medical condition. Dogs can help them remember to do that. These dogs are trained to know when the medications should be taken. They bring the medication to their humans at a given time. They can even bring water so their humans can swallow the pills.

Helping Military Men and Women

After serving in the military, many people suffer
from PTSD. This stress disorder occurs after
a scary event. Military men and women may
experience PTSD after fighting in a war. Other
people may have it after surviving or seeing an act
of violence. People with PTSD feel frightened or
depressed. They may have trouble sleeping.

**Fighting in a war often has lasting effects on a soldier's mental
health.**

A veteran of the Iraq War poses with her PTSD support dog.

Dogs who help people with PTSD are not service dogs. They are called support dogs. The animals can help keep people calm and help them feel safe. Support dogs are also good at following commands. These dogs can provide fun and companionship for people with PTSD. In addition, support dogs can help veterans who have injuries or other medical conditions.

Dogs can be very good listeners for kids who are learning to read.

Reader dogs are patient with struggling readers.

Eager Listeners

Many children have a hard time learning to read. They may also feel nervous about reading out loud. Reader dogs are special dogs that children can read to. Dogs are friendly and help the children relax. They do not make fun of mistakes, like other children might. Dogs pay attention and enjoy listening to the children's words.

The dogs make visits to schools and libraries. Through reader dog programs, children become more-confident readers at school and at home. Better reading skills help children in all their school subjects. The acceptance children feel from dogs can help them build self-esteem. Reader dogs, like all helping animals, have a wonderful way of making people's lives better. ★

A group of students pet their class's reading assistance dog.

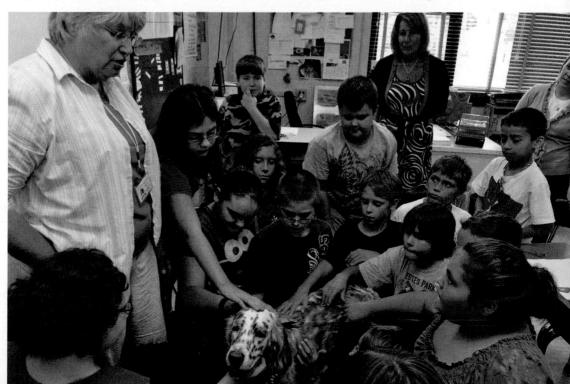

Number of people in the United States with seeing or hearing disabilities: 9.3 million

Number of people in the United States with difficulty walking, carrying objects, or climbing stairs: 21.2 million

Number of children with autism in the United States: 1 in 68

Number of people who use guide dogs in the United States and Canada: 10,000

Time it takes to train a service dog: 4 months to 1 year

Life span of a capuchin monkey: 30 to 40 years

Did you find the truth?

Horses can help guide people who are blind.

Dogs are never allowed in hospitals.

Resources

Books

Bozzo, Linda. *Guide Dog Heroes*. Berkeley Heights, NJ: Enslow Publishers, 2011.

Gregory, Josh. *Working Dogs*. New York: Children's Press, 2013.

Hoffman, Mary Ann. *Helping Dogs*. New York: Gareth Stevens, 2011.

Moore, Eva. *Buddy: The First Seeing Eye Dog*. New York: Scholastic, 1996.

Visit this Scholastic Web site for more information on animals helping at home:
★ www.factsfornow.scholastic.com
Enter the keywords **Animals Helping at Home**

Important Words

allergic (uh-LUR-jik) — having a reaction to certain foods or other items that causes sneezing, rashes, or trouble breathing

autism (AW-tiz-uhm) — a condition that causes someone to have trouble learning, communicating, and forming relationships with people

disabilities (dis-uh-BIL-i-teez) — conditions that prevent someone from being able to move easily or from being able to act or think in ways typically expected of a person

epilepsy (EP-uh-lep-see) — a disease of the brain that may cause a person to have sudden blackouts or to lose control of his or her movements

navigator (NAV-i-gate-ur) — a person in charge of finding where you are and where you need to go when traveling

paralyzed (PAR-uh-lyzd) — unable to move or feel part of the body

post-traumatic stress disorder (POHST-truh-MAT-ik STREHS dis-OR-dur) —also called PTSD; a psychiatric disorder that can occur after experiencing or witnessing life-threatening events such as military combat

seizures (SEE-zhurz) — sudden attacks or spasms

withers (WIH-thurz) — the ridge between the shoulder bones of a horse

Index

Page numbers in **bold** indicate illustrations.

About the Author

Lucia Raatma is a writer and editor who enjoys working on books for young readers. She earned a bachelor's degree in English from the University of South Carolina and a master's degree in cinema studies from New York University. She likes writing about all sorts of subjects including history, conservation, animals, and character education. She lives with her husband and their two children in the Tampa Bay area of Florida.